# This book belongs to:

_____

_____

Associate Publisher: Rebecca J. Razo
Art Director: Shelley Baugh
Project Manager: Sandy Phan
Senior Editor: Amanda Weston
Associate Editor: Stephanie Meissner
Production Designers: Debbie Aiken, Amanda Tannen
Production Manager: Nicole Szawlowski
Production Coordinator: Lawrence Marquez
Administrative Assistant: Kate Davidson

Step-by-step illustrations and doodled artwork by Stephanie Corfee
Written by Sandy Phan

www.walterfoster.com
3 Wrigley, Suite A
Irvine, CA 92618

1 3 5 7 9 10 8 6 4 2

I  Sweet Treats!

Activity Book

A yummy assortment of stickers, games, recipes, step-by-step drawing projects, and more to satisfy your sweet tooth!

Table of Contents

Sweet Treats

There are so many delicious sweet treats—cakes, cookies, candies, and more! How many tasty confections have you tried?

S'more

Gummy Bears

Cupcake

Gumdrops

Gingerbread
Man

Gumballs

Chocolate-dipped
Strawberry

Sugar Cookie

Macaroons

Box of Chocolates

Cake Pop

Chocolate Chip Cookie

Cotton Candy

Birthday Cake

Ice Cream Cone

Ice Cream Bar

Doughnut

YOU ROCK

U GO GIRL

Conversation Hearts

Jelly Beans

7

Popsicle

Sundae

Truffles

Lollipop

Candy Apple

Saltwater Taffy

Wedding Cake

8

Drawing Projects

Learn how to draw 12 different sweet treats by starting with basic shapes and then following step by simple step. Practice your drawings on scrap paper. Once you've mastered each dessert, you can add a finished colored drawing to the Sketch Pad beginning on page 79.

Getting Started

When you look closely at the drawings in this book, you'll notice that they're made up of basic shapes, such as circles, triangles, and rectangles. To draw all your favorite sweet treats, just start with simple shapes as you see here. It's easy and fun!

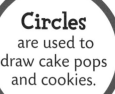

Circles are used to draw cake pops and cookies.

Rectangles are good for ice cream sandwiches.

Triangles are great for pie and cake slices.

Drawing Exercises

Before you begin, warm up your hand
by drawing squiggles and shapes.

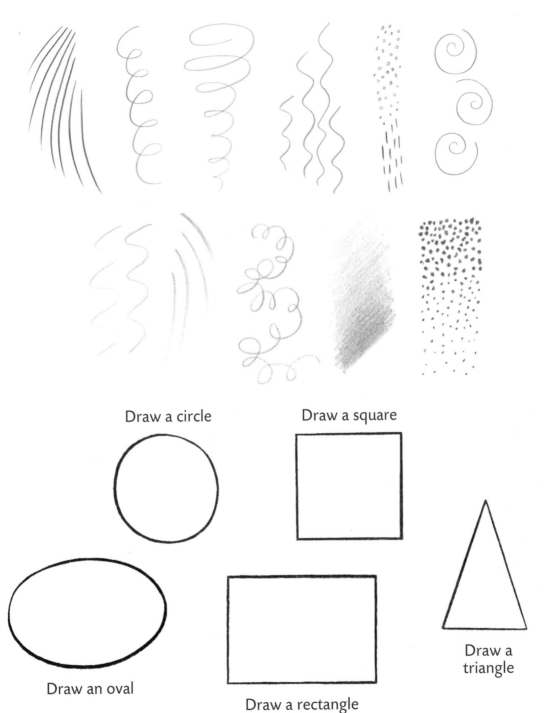

Draw a circle

Draw a square

Draw an oval

Draw a rectangle

Draw a triangle

Combining Shapes

Most of your drawings will use more than one basic shape, like the candy and brownie sundae below. Now look at the things around you. What basic shapes do you see?

Colors and Flavors

Here are just a few flavors you can create with color. What other flavors can you think of for each color?

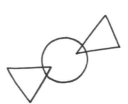

Red = Strawberry

Orange = Orange

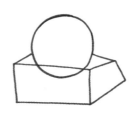

Yellow = Lemon

Green = Mint

Blue = Blueberry

Purple = Grape

White = Vanilla

Black = Licorice

Brown = Chocolate

Sweet Doodles

Sweets come in all shapes and patterns, including hearts, stars, spirals, and stripes. Practice doodling all the different sweets you can think of using the Sketch Pad beginning on page 79.

Hearts

Stars

Swirls

Sprinkles

Spirals

Zigzags

Gingerbread Man

The gingerbread man is a great holiday treat. You can make his face, clothes, and buttons with candy and frosting for extra sweetness!

Fun Fact

The first gingerbread men were created in the 16th century. Queen Elizabeth I gave her important guests gingerbread cakes. People also make gingerbread in the shape of animals and houses, like the witch's house in the fairy tale "Hansel and Gretel."

Chocolate-covered Strawberry

Strawberries can be dipped in white, milk, or dark chocolate. Sometimes, they are also decorated with nuts and candy.

4

5

6

Fun Fact Covering anything in chocolate makes it tasty. People dip many different foods in chocolate—from cookies and crackers to bacon and chili peppers!

Cupcake

A cupcake is a small cake baked in a cup. Cupcakes come in oh-so-many yummy flavors and toppings!

4

5

6

Fun Fact

In Britain, cupcakes are called fairy cakes because they are small and can be served at a "fairy" party.

Fruit Parfait

A parfait is a dessert made up of layers of ice cream or yogurt and fruit. It is served in a tall glass.

Fun Fact

In French, *parfait* (pronounced "par-fay") means "perfect." What could be more perfect than layers of sweet goodness in one glass?

Birthday Cake

A birthday cake is shared with family and friends
to celebrate growing another year older.
So make a birthday wish, and blow out the candles!

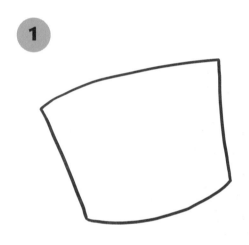

Fun Fact

Ancient Greeks made the first birthday cakes.
They brought moon-shaped honey cakes to the temple
of Artemis, who was the goddess of wild animals and the moon.

Root Beer Float

Also called a "black cow," this fun and fizzy treat comes with smooth vanilla ice cream and foamy root beer.

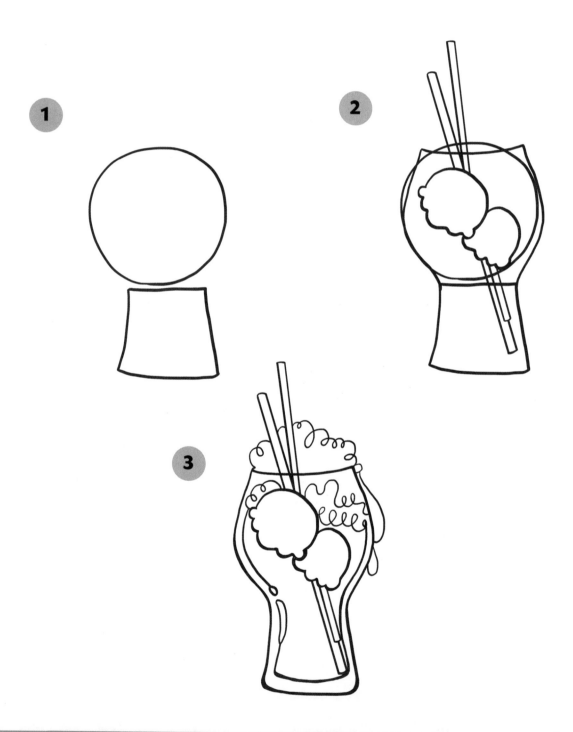

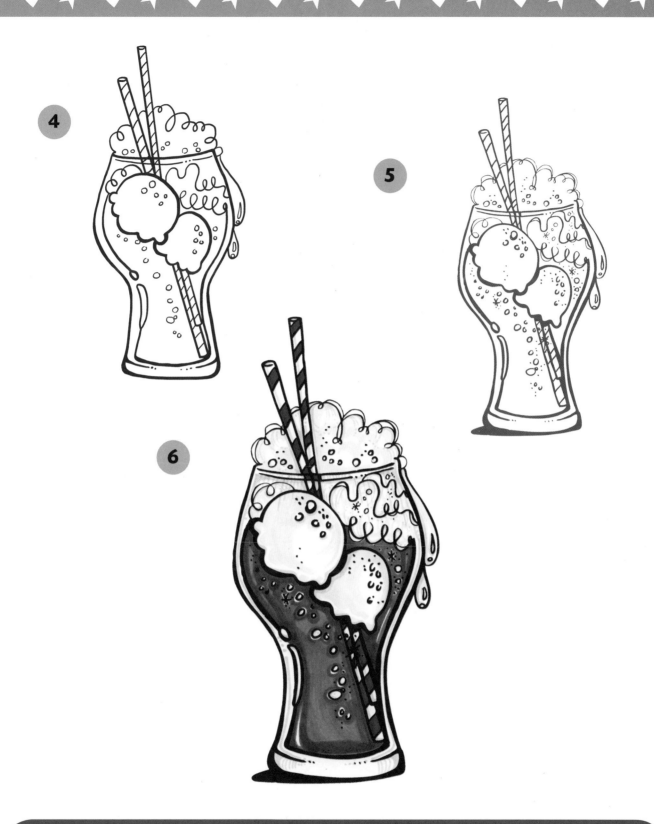

Fun Fact

The root beer flavor comes from herbs, roots, oils, and sugar. Before root beer became a popular soda, people used many of the same ingredients for medicine and tea. One pharmacist sold it as a miracle cure!

Strawberry Shortcake

Serve this summertime sweet at your next tea party. Your friends will love the spongy cake and juicy strawberries topped with fluffy whipped cream.

1

2

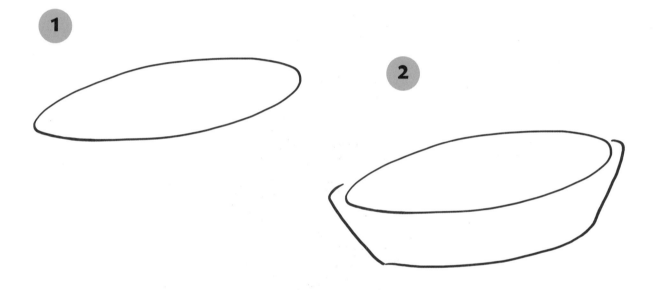

3

Fun Fact

The original shortcake began in Europe as a sweet, crumbly biscuit. Americans added fresh strawberries and started throwing shortcake parties in 1850 to celebrate summertime. Today, most people use sponge cake or white angel-food cake in strawberry shortcake.

Candy Apple

Candy apples are made by dipping an apple-on-a-stick in melted sugar, toffee, caramel, or chocolate. They are called caramel apples when they are made with caramel, like this one!

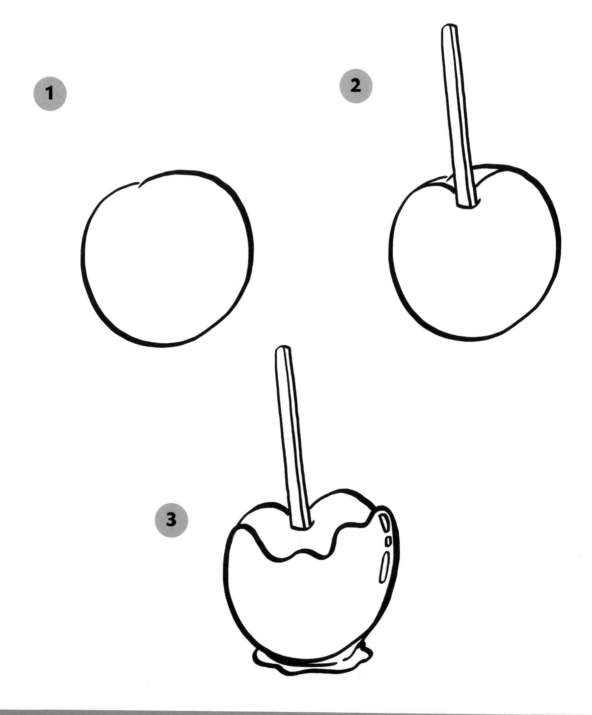

1

2

3

Fun Fact

Candy apples are known as toffee or taffy apples in Britain. In France, they are called *les pommes d'amour,* or apples of love, because of the traditional red candy coating. Candy-apple red is a bright red color often found on cars, nail polish, and even guitars!

Banana Split

Split this sweet treat with a friend ... unless you can finish a banana, three scoops of ice cream, tons of toppings, whipped cream, chopped nuts, and a cherry all by yourself!

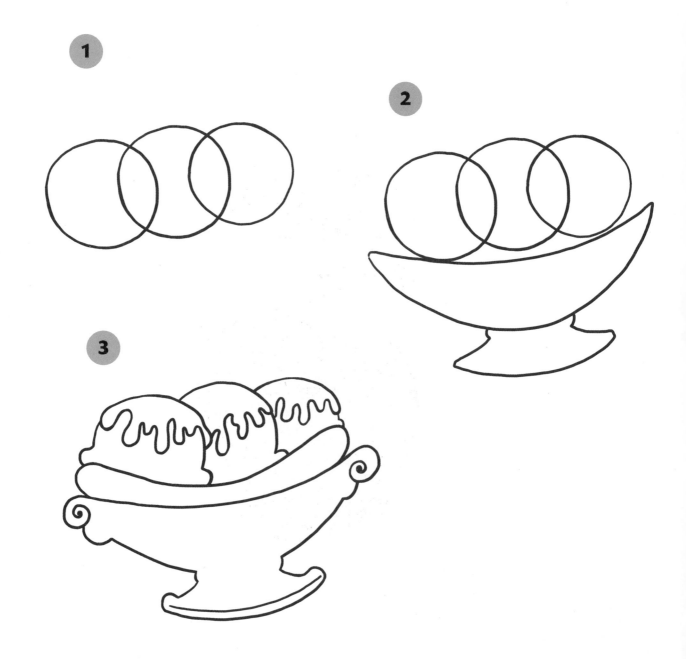

Fun Fact

The Banana Split Festival is held every year in Wilmington, Ohio. The festival features a banana split eating contest and has a "Make Your Own Banana Split" booth. Legend has it the banana split was invented in a Wilmington eatery.

Box of Chocolates

Reach into a box of chocolates for a sweet surprise! You may find a white, milk, or dark chocolate filled with caramel, nuts, mint, fruit, or another yummy filling.

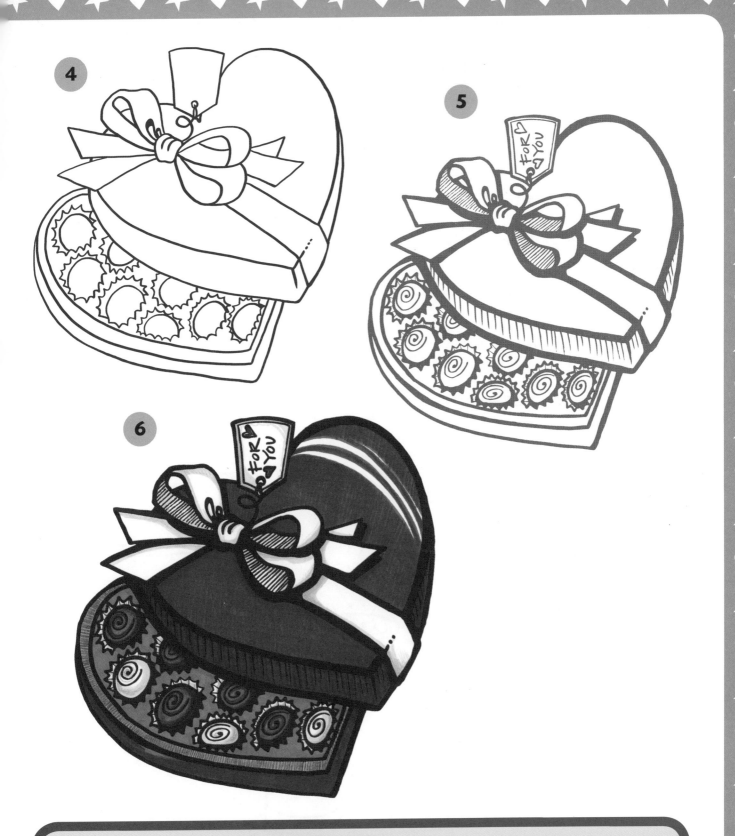

Fun Fact

"Chocolate" comes from the Aztec word *xocoatl,* meaning "bitter water." The Aztecs believed the cacao plant came from their god Quetzalcoatl, and they drank chocolate for magical strength. They also used the cacao bean as money.

Wedding Cake

A wedding cake is a sweet symbol of a couple's love. The bride and groom share this beautiful treat with friends and family on their special day.

Fun Fact

In medieval England, guests stacked sweet buns and breads between the bride and groom. If the couple could kiss over the pile without knocking it down, it meant they would have many children.

S'more

A s'more is a toasted marshmallow and a piece of chocolate sandwiched between two graham crackers. It's sticky, sweet, creamy, and crispy!

Fun Fact

The s'more was invented around a campfire in the early 1900s. In 1927, the first s'more recipe was published in the Girl Scout Handbook. S'more is short for "some more," because who can eat just one?

Sweet Treat Recipes

Learn how to make your own tasty treats!
Ask an adult for help, and then follow these easy
recipes for cupcakes, cookies, fudge, and more.

Vanilla Cupcakes

♥ Ingredients:

1 ½ sticks unsalted butter
1 ½ cups sugar
2 eggs
2 teaspoons vanilla extract
2 ½ teaspoons baking powder
¼ teaspoon salt
2 ½ cups flour
1 ¼ cups milk

Directions:

1. Preheat oven to 350 degrees Fahrenheit. Line a cupcake pan with paper liners.

2. Put butter in a mixing bowl and beat at medium speed until soft and creamy. Mix in the sugar. Then add eggs and beat well. Add the vanilla, baking powder, salt, flour, and milk. Mix batter until smooth.

3. Fill cupcake liners ⅔ full of batter. Do not overfill, as batter will rise. Bake 20 minutes or until toothpick stuck in center comes out clean.

4. Cool 10 minutes in pan, and then remove from pan. Place on wire rack to cool completely.

5. When the cupcakes have cooled, add your favorite frosting and toppings.

Fudge-a-Licious Squares

♥ Ingredients:

1 can (14 ounces) sweetened condensed milk
2 cups semisweet chocolate chips (12 ounces)
1 cup milk chocolate chips (6 ounces)
2 tablespoons butter
1 teaspoon vanilla
1 cup chopped pecans or walnuts (optional)

Directions:

1. Lightly grease a 9-inch square pan; line with a piece of plastic wrap about 18 to 24 inches in length, leaving the ends out to cover the finished fudge. The ends will also serve as "handles," which will help you lift the fudge out of the pan.

2. Heat the condensed milk, chocolate chips, butter, and vanilla in a double boiler over simmering water. Stir until the chocolate is melted, and the mixture is smooth.

3. Stir in nuts (optional) and pour into the prepared pan.

4. Spread mixture gently across the pan; then cover lightly with the ends of the plastic wrap.

5. Chill until firm. Lift out of the pan using the "handles," and cut into small squares.

Gingerbread Cookies

♥ Ingredients:

1 cup shortening
1 cup sugar
1 egg
3/4 cup molasses
2 tablespoons vinegar
5 cups flour
1 1/2 teaspoons baking soda
1/2 teaspoon salt
2-3 teaspoons ginger
1 teaspoon cinnamon
1 teaspoon cloves

Directions:

1. Cream together the shortening and sugar.

2. Beat in egg, molasses, and vinegar.

3. Sift together flour, baking soda, salt, ginger, cinnamon, and cloves.

4. Blend with the shortening mixture.

5. Chill in fridge for 3 hours.

6. Roll dough 1/2-inch thick and cut with cookie cutter. (For Cookie Ornaments, see instructions on page 46.)

7. Place on slightly greased cookie sheet, and bake at 375 degrees Fahrenheit for 5 minutes.

Chocolate Cupcakes

♥ **Ingredients:**

2 cups all-purpose flour

2 cups sugar

1/2 teaspoon baking powder

1 teaspoon salt

1 teaspoon baking soda

1/2 cup shortenting

1/3 cup water

2 large eggs

1/3 cup milk

1 teaspoon vanilla

4 ounces melted unsweetened
baking chocolate

Directions:

1. Preheat oven to 350 degrees Fahrenheit. Line cupcake pans with paper liners.

2. Combine all cupcake ingredients in a large mixing bowl. Mix at low speed for 30 seconds. Scrape bowl, and mix at high speed for 3 minutes.

3. Fill liners 1/2 to 2/3 full of batter. Bake 20-25 minutes or until toothpick inserted in center comes out clean.

4. Cool 10 minutes in pan, then remove from pan and place on wire rack to cool completely.

5. Spread top with chocolate frosting, and add candy shapes or your favorite toppings.

Strawberry Smoothie

♥ Ingredients:

2 ice cubes

1 cup low-fat milk

1/3 cup vanilla yogurt

2/3 cup frozen strawberries

1 1/2 teaspoon honey

1 teaspoon vanilla extract

Directions:

1. Put all of the ingredients in the blender.

2. Place the lid on the blender tightly. Blend for about one minute or until smooth.

3. Pour your strawberry smoothie into a glass. You can add a fresh strawberry on top, if you like.

Sweet Treat Crafts

Spread your love of all things sweet!
These crafty ideas will help you share the gift of
sweetness and throw a perfect party.

Paper Cone Party Favors

Give each of your guests a sweet treat to take home.

♥ **Materials:**

Patterned paper

Scissors

Ribbon

Candy

Directions:

1. Cut patterned paper into 5-inch squares. Make sure the paper has a pattern on both sides. If the paper is blank on one side, cut it into 10-inch x 5-inch rectangles. Fold the rectangles in half, so the pattern faces out on both sides.

2. Roll each square into a cone and tie a ribbon around it.

3. Put your favorite candy inside, and give these cones as party gifts.

Sweet Valentine

Make your Valentine's Day super sweet with these cards.

♥ **Materials:**

Colored paper

Scissors

Colored pencils or crayons

Ribbon (optional)

Heart-shaped doilies (optional)

Foam hearts (optional)

Glitter glue (optional)

Directions:

1. Cut a heart out of colored paper with scissors.

2. Use colored pencils or crayons to write your Valentine's message. You may also decorate your card with ribbon, a heart-shaped doily, foam hearts, or glitter glue.

3. Now add a sweet treat to your Valentine card! Here are a few ideas:
   - Punch a hole in your card and attach a heart-shaped lollipop with a ribbon.
   - Put your card in an envelope with heart-shaped candy or chocolate.

Cookie Ornaments

♥ **Materials:**

Gingerbread cookies

Straw

Ribbon

Directions:

1. Make gingerbread cookies in different shapes (see recipe on page 40). Before baking the cookies, use a straw to make a hole in the top of each cookie.

2. After the cookies have been baked and cooled, string an 8-inch piece of ribbon through each cookie.

3. Tie together the ends of the ribbon, and add a bow if you like. Hang your cookie ornaments as decorations or wrap them up as gifts.

Sweet Treat Fun!

Grab a pen, markers, or crayons and get ready for some fun and super sweet activities!

Sweet Treats Trivia

How much do you know about sweet treats?
Test your sweets IQ with these trivia questions.

1 What is the most popular ice cream flavor?
    A. Chocolate
    B. Vanilla
    C. Strawberry
    D. Rocky Road

2 When did people start chewing gum?
    A. 500 years ago
    B. 50 years ago
    C. Thousands of years ago
    D. 100 years ago

3 What was the first candy made from?
    A. Honey, nuts, and fruit
    B. Sugar and nuts
    C. Chocolate and nuts
    D. Chocolate and sugar

4 What is the difference between a cobbler and a pie?

5 Which country eats the most chocolate?

6 How much did the world's largest cream puff weigh?

7 What were the first cakes like?

8 How do you make caramel?

9 What were marshmallows originally used for?

10 How old was the inventor of popsicles?

Sweet Treat Trivia Answers

1. **B. Vanilla**
2. **C. Thousands of years ago** (Ancient Greeks and Mayans chewed natural gum found in trees.)
3. **A. Honey, nuts, and fruit**
4. **A cobbler has no bottom crust.**
5. **Switzerland**
6. **More than 125 pounds!** (It was baked for the 2011 Wisconsin State Fair. The cream puff is Wisconsin's official state dessert.)
7. **Bread sweetened with honey** (Ancient Egyptians were the first bakers to make this sweet treat. Today, cakes are softer, because they have many small air bubbles inside.)
8. **By heating sugar until it turns brown.**
9. **To soothe sore throats.** (The juice of the marsh mallow plant had healing properties. Today, marshmallows don't contain marsh mallow sap.)
10. **Eleven** (In 1905, Frank Epperson mixed soda powder and water. He left the stirring stick in the cup and forgot it outside. The next morning, he found a frozen pop.)

Sweet Shoppe Menu

Have you ever wanted to be a chef that gets to bake yummy desserts? Fill in the blanks on this menu and get creative deciding the tasty treats and drinks you will serve your customers. Maybe you'll be tempted to have a taste test too!

_____'s
(your name)

Sweet Shoppe Menu

Hours

_____ through _____
(day)   (day)

___am/pm to ___am/pm
(time)   (time)

Delectably Decadent Desserts

_____Pie

_____-Style Cheesecake

_____Mousse

Chocolate_____

_____Pound Cake

_____Doughnut

_____Danish

_____Cake

_____ Tart with _____ Sauce

_____ Pie with _____ Crust

_____Cream Pudding

_____Cobbler

_____Ice Cream

SWEET SAVINGS

Buy one

_____,

get one

_____

FREE!

Draw a picture of your free menu item here.

Scrumptiously Sweet Drinks

_____ Juice Cooler

_____ Punch

Sparkling _____ Cider with a _____ Twist

Strawberry _____

_____Float

_____Soda

_____Lemonade

_____Tea

_____ Spice Fizz

_____ Shake

Mint_____

Ice Cream Creations

Make up your own ice cream flavors. Then color the scoops and fill in the names of your new flavors.

Tasty Toppings

Add loads of toppings to the cupcake below using crayons, markers, or colored pencils.

A Sweet Surprise

Complete this story alone or with friends, taking turns filling in the blanks. Read it aloud when you are finished to hear the sweet, silly story you created!

One _____ day, _____ ran out of _____. She mixed
      adjective   girl's name   sweet food

_____ with _____ and _____. Then she _____ed
   sweet food   sweet food   sweet food   verb

_____ sauce on top. It was so _____, _____ made this
    flavor   adjective   same name

_____ treat to _____ with friends and family. Soon, _____'s
   adjective   verb   same name

dessert became very _____. Everyone _____ed her for the recipe.
                        adjective   verb

That year, _____ entered her dessert in the Most _____ Dessert Contest.
             same name   adjective

The winner would receive _____ dollars and her recipe would be _____ed
                            number   verb

in the _____ _____ cookbook. _____ was very _____,
         adjective   noun   same name   adjective

but her friends and family believed she could _____ the contest.
                                                  verb

The judges thought _____'s dessert was _____ and _____. She
                     same name   adjective   adjective

won first place! When the judges asked her the name of her sweet treat, she said it was called the

_____ _____ _____.
  adjective   color   animal

Sweet Treats Personality Quiz

Which sweet treat are you—cotton candy, pumpkin pie, candy apple, or ice cream sundae? Take this quiz to find out!

1 Which color do you like best?
A. Orange
B. Pink
C. I can't choose. I like all colors!
D. Red

2 What types of stories do you like?
A. Adventures
B. Fairy tales
C. I love all kinds of stories.
D. Scary stories

3 Where do you love to go for fun?
A. The park
B. An amusement park or carnival
C. The beach
D. The mall

4 What do you like to do with your friends?
   A. Play outdoors.
   B. Make sweet treats together.
   C. Anything and everything, as long as we're doing it together.
   D. Tell ghost stories or paint each other's nails.

5 What are your favorite shoes?
   A. Comfy sneakers
   B. Dressy sandals
   C. Flip flops
   D. Stylish boots

What type of sweet treat are you? Quiz Answers

Mostly As: Pumpkin Pie. You are bold and adventurous, with a hint of sweet spice. Your friends know they can count on you for great game ideas.

Mostly Bs: Cotton Candy. You are lighthearted and super sweet. Like the fairy tales you love, you bring a bit of magic to everyone around you.

Mostly Cs: Ice Cream Sundae. You bring together all the best flavors, just like an ice cream sundae! Your friends love having fun in the sun—or doing just about anything—with you.

Mostly Ds: Candy Apple. You are fearless, like a fiery red candy apple. Your friends come to you for fashion advice and spine-chilling scary stories.

Making Sweets Crossword Puzzle

Across

1. A tool for whipping eggs or cream.
4. A mixture of egg whites and sugar beaten until fluffy and stiff; used to top pastry or pies. Lemon _____ pie.
5. A tool with sharp edges for turning cookie dough into different shapes.
6. A sweet mixture for coating, decorating or filling cakes, cookies, and other treats; icing.
8. _____ spoons are used to add the correct amount of an ingredient when baking.
9. A row or level on a cake. Wedding cakes usually have _____s.
11. Sugar or syrup heated until it turns brown; used as a sauce, flavoring, or coating.
12. A spice made from the bark of tropical Asian trees; used to flavor treats. _____ roll.
13. A powder made from ground grain; used to make bread, cakes, and pastry.
14. A cream beaten until light and fluffy; used as a topping on sweet treats.
15. _____ powder is a key ingredient in chocolate milkshakes.

Down

2. A sweet, sticky, gold liquid made by bees from the nectar of flowers; used to sweeten treats.
3. A thick, sweet liquid poured over pancakes and waffles.
4. A white, pillow-like treat made of sugar and gelatin. A _____ is a key ingredient in s'mores.
5. Baked pastry shell used to hold pie fillings.
7. Different colored candy bits for topping doughnuts, cupcakes, or cookies.
10. A flavor that comes from a bean; the most popular ice cream flavor.
12. Small, cone-shaped pieces often used in cookies. They come in different flavors, including chocolate, butterscotch, and white chocolate.

Answers on page 96.

Hansel & Gretel Maze

Help Hansel and Gretel find their way to the witch's candy house!

Start

Finish

Solution on page 96.

Sweet Bites Haikus

Haiku poems began in Japan, but today, they are popular around the world. Haikus are very short poems with three lines. The first line has 5 syllables, the second line has 7 syllables, and the last line has 5 syllables. Sometimes, the first and last lines rhyme.

Example of a Haiku

Sticky on my chin
Magic melting on my tongue
Sweet cloud of cotton

Write a haiku about one of the sweet treats you learned how to draw from the list to the right, or come up with sweet subjects of your own.

Banana split
Birthday cake
Box of chocolates
Candy apple
Chocolate-covered strawberry
Cupcake
Fruit parfait
Gingerbread man
Root beer float
S'more
Strawberry shortcake
Wedding cake

Title: _____

(5) _____
(7) _____
(5) _____

Title: _____

(5) _____
(7) _____
(5) _____

Title: _____

(5) _____
(7) _____
(5) _____

Candy Word Search

Candy comes in all shapes, sizes, and flavors. See if you can find all the candy words in the word search. Words can go up and down, backwards and forwards, or diagonally.

```
M Z G U M M Y B E A R S J K B M S I L M J Q D Z C
L H U S T N R O C K C A N D Y Y N H E S Q K R A K
T R M B X I Z L O Q P N P G F Q A M M L R Q P X T
D W L I C O R I C E F K H F A U U D O T C R O X O
C I H G P X S S L R F K A S I G F X N V P O I T N
A S B P J Y C W V E U T U W E H L V D R N H O J X
N Y U B B B M Y X V Q I A L Z O Z H R O W X R C J
D I T M G W U J N O G R B L R I G D O B P M Y A R
Y L T M U D B T A U C B F S L S J L P D J H U R E
C U E R M X K O M S U G C O T T O N C A N D Y A M
A J R M V O T Z I B P R E A M I D K O L I H G M X
N F S K Y V Y P N P E A N U T B R I T T L E V E I
E H C N H M K H T D U W Z E Y C A N D Y B A R L C
P X O L M A R S H M A L L O W M W E D Y S Y Q T I
L X T L O L L I P O P N U D A F U D G E D E E E B
K L C N A R Z R P U W Z S U J E L L Y B E A N S B
P A H J E T R U F F L E V W X Z D O B H V I I W W
```

Candy cane	**Taffy**	**Bubble gum**	**Peanut brittle**
Rock candy	**Cotton candy**	**Fudge**	**Mint**
Jelly beans	**Caramel**	**Lemon drop**	**Butterscotch**
Gummy bears	**Lollipop**	**Truffle**	**Candy bar**
Licorice		**Marshmallow**	

Answers on page 96.

I Love Sweet Treats! Diary

From the cold and creamy to the chocolaty and dreamy, what's not to love about sweet treats? This diary is a delicious place for you to gush about the desserts that tickle your taste buds and show your delight for anything that brings bliss to your sweet senses!

Your Sweet Cravings

Most mouth-watering cookies

_____
_____
_____
_____

Yummiest candies

_____
_____
_____
_____

Favorite flavors

_____
_____
_____
_____

Tastiest treats

_____
_____
_____
_____

Sweetest memory

_____
_____
_____
_____
_____
_____
_____
_____
_____

What I like best about sweet treats

_____
_____
_____
_____
_____
_____
_____
_____
_____
_____
_____
_____
_____

Simply Scrumptious!

Use these pages to paste in pics of the most delectable desserts you can find—they can be of sweets you've tasted or of treats you'd like to try!

Crazy Cake Collage

What are the coolest, craziest, most creative cakes ever made? Make a collage of the images you find in old magazines or online.

Delicious Doodles

Ready to get creative with your cravings?
Decorate these pages with your sweet doodles!

Tasty Tales

Tell a story starring a sweet treat here. You can write about the first time you tasted a favorite sweet, describe a time you shared a treat with someone you love, or make up a story from the point of view of a pastry!

_____

_____

_____

_____

_____

_____

_____

_____

_____

_____

_____

_____

_____

_____

_____

_____

Sweets Around the World

Every country has its unique desserts, such as Italian gelato, Japanese mochi, and French éclairs. Decorate these pages with images of international sweet treats you find in old magazines or online.

Sweet Recipes

Use these pages to jot down easy dessert recipes you can dish up. Look in magazines and online, or ask a family member for a favorite treat that you can make together!

Frosting Fantasy

Decorate the cake!

Sketch Pad

Now that you have practiced drawing all of your favorite sweet treats step by step on scrap paper, you can fill the pages of this sketch pad with finished colored drawings and doodles. You can even decorate your scenes with stickers from the back of this book!

Puzzle Answers

Page 58: Making Sweets

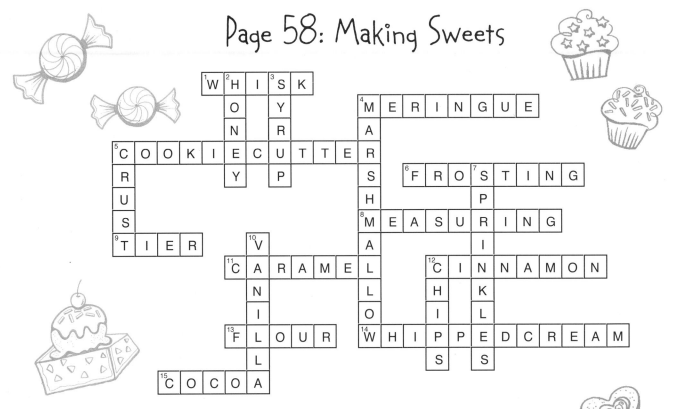

Crossword solution:
- 1 Across: WHISK
- 4 Across: MERINGUE
- 5 Across: COOKIECUTTER
- 6 Across: FROSTING
- 8 Across: MEASURING
- 9 Across: TIER
- 11 Across: CARAMEL
- 12 Across: CINNAMON
- 13 Across: FLOUR
- 14 Across: WHIPPEDCREAM
- 15 Across: COCOA
- 2 Down: HONEY
- 3 Down: SYRUP
- Down: MARSHMALLOW
- 7 Down: SPICING / TIPPINGS
- 10 Down: VANILLA
- Down: CRUST
- 12 Down: CHILLS
- Down: MIXERS

Page 59: Hansel & Gretel Maze

Page 62: Candy Word Search

```
M Z G U M M Y B E A R S J K B M S I L M J Q D Z C
L H U S T N R O C K C A N D Y Y N H E S Q K R A K
T R M B X I Z L O Q P N P G F Q A M M O T C R O X O
D W L I C O R I C E F K H F A U U D N T C R O X O
C I H G P X S S L R F K A S I G F X N V P O I T N
A S B P J Y C W V E U T U W E H L V D R N H O J X
N Y I B B B M Y X V Q I A L Z O Z H R O W X R C J
D I T M G W U J N O G R B L R I G D O B P M Y A R
Y L U M U D B T A U C B F S L S J L P D J H U E A
C U E R M X K O M S U G C O T T O N C A N D Y M M
A J S M V O T Z I B P R E A M I D K O L I H G E X
N F K Y V V Y P N T P E A N U T B R I T T L E V I
E H C N H M K H T D U W Z E Y C A N D Y B A R L C
P X O L M A R S H M A L L O W M W E D Y S Y Q T I
L X T L O L L I P O P N U D A F U D G E D E E E B
K L C N A R Z R P U W Z S U G J E L L Y B E A N S B
P A H J E T R U F F L E V W X Z D O B H V I I W W
```

Get a grown-up to help you cut out these fun accessories!

Come on in!

...especially if you have sweet treats!

Gobble up a great read!

Books are treats for the brain.

Savor the
sweet taste
of a good
book!

Do not Disturb!
(Taking time out for a treat.)

I ♥ Sweet Treats!

Recipe for: _____

Ingredients:

Recipe for: _____

Ingredients:

Recipe for: _____

Ingredients:

Recipe for: _____

Ingredients:

Directions:

Directions:

Directions:

Directions:

sweets for
my sweet

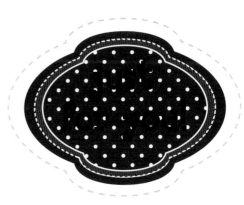

just
for you

thinking
of you

with love

baked
with love

treats
for you

To: _____
From: _____

To: _____
From: _____

To: _____
From: _____

To: _____
From: _____

To: _____
From: _____

To: _____
From: _____

To: _____
From: _____

To: _____
From: _____

To: _____
From: _____

To: _____
From: _____

To: _____
From: _____

To: _____
From: _____

Decorate these postcards and mail them to a friend!

Place
Stamp
Here

_____
_____
_____

Place
Stamp
Here

_____
_____
_____